The Shithouse Trouble

of

Irv Fugman, Deceased

william frank

TUCKFORD BUNNY PRESS

ISBN-13: 979-8-218-04970-6

Printed in the United States of America.
First Printing: August 14, 2022
Second Printing: February 19, 2023

Other books by William Frank:

The Fulgent Requiem (2021)
Slumgullion (2019)
The Purgatory Elm (2018)
Yuneko (2015)
Fiasco Galante (2014)
The Encolpia (2011)
The Morphine Fawn (2009)

All Tuckford Bunny books are available at Amazon.com
and other retailers.

About Tuckford Bunny Press
Tuckford Bunny Press is a private, make-believe
company that publishes the literary works of William
Frank. It is the only imaginary Press that will publish
such funny-headed little books.

Acknowledgements

Floral designs on the Book's back cover, Title page and Memorial page used from the Permission-Free Designs in the book Art Nouveau Motifs, Dover Publications, Inc, Mineola, NY, 2002.

Irv Fugman Skull image on the book cover and the Seal of the Department of the Dead in the Burial Permit used from the Permission-Free Designs in the book Mythological & Fantastic Creatures, from Dover Publications, Inc, Mineola, NY, 2002. A little amateur photoshopping removed the stovepipe hat from the figure on the cover.

The Cat under the Umbrella image is from a photo taken by the author of a little flag that originally read *Welcome* that my upstairs neighbor placed in the garden outside our doors. Naturally, I fudged it up some.

About the Author:

William Frank, an author of eight books of poetry, is a man with an amiable façade, a witless disregard for reasonable care and a personal nimbus almost nine feet high. His work has previously appeared in *The Dillydoun Review,* the Bards Annual 2022 and he was a runner-up for the 2008 *Discovery/The Boston Review* prize offered by the 92nd Street Y.

When not writing poetry, he enjoys long hours of losing at chess, bingeing on 1950's Japanese Cinema, summering with the Devil, punching cryptids in the face and Kulning.

Contents

And there's another country
  I've heard of long ago
Most dear to them that love her,
  Most great to them that know.

We may not count her armies,
  We may not see her King;
Her fortress is a faithful heart,
  Her pride is suffering.

And soul by soul and silently
  Her shining bounds increase
And her ways are ways of gentleness
  And all her paths are peace.

I Vow to Thee, My Country
Cecil Spring-Rice

In Loving Memory
of
Irv Fugman

He will be missed by all who knew him: the feral cats of Lentil County and Sherman Melty, the last semi-lucid member of The Bottle Cap Collecting Club, two parties he fed and bathed. A man who was better than us all, may he ascend into Heaven on bright wings of transcendent glory, despite his rumored super-gonorrhea, a rumor this community would do well not to shamelessly repeat.

I Told Fred to Let Me Run This Damned Department...

The Lentil County Department of the Dead
The Mort Mission Bureau of Records & Statistics
Burial-Cremation-Transport Permit

No. 194453672008   **Date:** October 10, 2023

This permit shall also be handed to the Keeper of the Cemetery or Crematorium by The Lentil County Director of the Dead or the Mort Mission Clerk representing the Director.

The Certificate of Death having been furnished to this Department, as required by the Sanitary Code and the Mortal Codes of our County, permission is hereby given to *Mr. Groomer Gruddy c/o Mortal Transport, Inc. of 727 Capt. Wuenschel Drive, Tucker Town* to remove the remains of:

Mr./Mrs./Other: Irving Fug
Aged: 64 Yrs.   3 Months   16 Days
who died at *The Lentil County Community Hospital* on *October 9, 2023* from HOSPITAL/CHAPEL for Burial/Cremation at *The Lentil County Cemetery of Perpetual Grace* on *October 10, 2023*

Jarmuz Klemer, MD
Lickmer Weltz
Mort Mission Clerk, #24529088
The Department of the Dead

The Seal of the Department of the Dead

The Mort Mission Clerk

It has been my misfortune to shoulder all the blame
  as the Lentil County Mort Mission Clerk
  in charge of all the burial transport paperwork
for the failures, dereliction, incompetence and shame

that comes with all the errors that were made
  in shipping Irv Fugman to his final resting place
  in The Lentil Cemetery of Perpetual Grace
which has made me consider *my* prospects and be afraid,

why can't I have a mind and heart that's sound?
Why can't I stop drinking and fooling around
  or take more care in the work I do?

Each morning, my manager dresses me down
as Irv Fugman's corpse goes all over town
  and presents his livid lechery to you.

Burial at The Lentil Cemetery of Perpetual Grace

As I was later told (I did not attend)
  in the first of many punches to the head,
  at the gravesite, there somewhat soberly gathered
moirologists, a squirrel, the Reverend

and a few girls from the bar where the priest misbehaved,
  and after six hours in the rain with no coffin in sight
  it finally erupted in a cataclysmic fight
until the big girl with the lisp fell into the grave.

Wet, muddy, preternaturally big-chested,
she was quite a pound of butter to try and rescue
  and despite the best efforts they could do

not only could they not get her disinterred
but then the priest fell in on top of her
  where it all got seamy and everyone was arrested.

Irv Fugman at the Fresco Hotel

When he arrived instead at the Fresco Hotel
  baked into his suit, peaceful and green,
  his makeup a mess, his face drawn and lean
but rakish despite looking so unwell,

though Management could see he desperately needed rest,
  lying as he was face down in the lobby,
  still, unsympathetic, continentally snobby,
Lorenz informed Irv he was upsetting all the guests

and he would either have to leave the Fresco immediately
or take the Beaumont Margrave Suite
  at nine hundred and fifty dollars a night

which, he sniffed, was the only current vacancy.
When Irv paltered, they threw him into the street
  after a decidedly one-sided fight.

An Entirely Understandable Human Mistake

I'm no different from anyone else, to be sure,
   I'm certainly not paid like I'm divine and infallible
   and just like every human slob, I'm susceptible
to accidents, boredom, cramps and Force Majeure,

whose record could survive an investigation?
   So maybe everyone should shut their fat face
   and conduct themselves with some humility and grace
and help me find the corpse before it spreads contagion,

clogs a sewer, snarls traffic, ends up in someone's lunch,
causes blonde heart attacks in those with sensitivities
   or otherwise brings the county to its knees.

If you *need* a confession, the paperwork got smudged
by a little square of pecan-crusted fudge
   I shouldn't be eating because of my diabetes.

4

Crisis at the Lentil County Department of the Dead

It didn't help that I came into the office with a twinge.
  Naturally, the hysterical search was on
  to find out where the corpse had gone
with everyone's tits out and unhinged.

We had a department meeting and then a break,
  then a planning meeting and then broke into groups,
  stopped for lunch and then marshalled the troops
into a meeting to discuss the steps we'd take

to canvas the town, field inquiries and address
the police department, civic leaders and the press,
  and agreed I was a fat imbecile and to blame for it all

and then everyone went out for happy hour at Malone's.
I was at Burt's desk licking his wife's picture when the phone
  to my relief brought a welcome call...

The Pugnacious Arrest of Irv Fugman

After being beaten up for drunkenness, vagrancy and soliciting,
   fighting at the Fresco and threatening guests,
   blocking a bus lane and resisting arrest,
the police brought Irv downtown for questioning

til one detective thought he saw this in another county,
   what with his algid personality and the flies,
   suggesting that Irv may have spitefully died
and after eight hours of silence, finally called me.

At last I thought I shipped him to the Cemetery
but to my utter horror and exasperation
   someone downstairs misheard the destination

which they said sounded something like ferry
and put him on a shuttle to the Isle of the Shades
   where they were holding their annual Hot Pants Parade.

Grand Marshal Fugman at the Hot Pants Parade

The ferry was a disaster, as you'd expect:
    They accused Irv Fugman of being a pervert
    shamelessly looking up every woman's skirt,
a rictus of twisted joy laying there on the deck

so that when they reached the Isle of the Shades
    they pummeled him and kicked him across the floor,
    lifted him by his pants and threw him overboard
and he crashed into a booth selling lemonade

from which he was shoved onto a passing float,
a Banana on wheels like a giant sundae boat,
    and as the only one that day wearing a suit,

they lobbed poor Irv onto the Marshal's throne,
put hot pants on his head and, like a baffled scone,
    he rode like a squashy monarch down the route.

Irv Fugman and the Strawberry Balloon

After the Banana finished its run
   they left him on the float so they could dance
   up and down the street in their hot pants
banging pots and pans while he crisped in the sun.

I think he would have cried could any tears be shed.
   He just sat there like a sagging green festoon
   until he tangled in the ropes of a hot air balloon
struggling with their blast valve overhead

and over the joyous music of the fair,
snared by the balloon, he flew through the air
   and, beyond the singing crowd, crossed the sea

until the wind blew them back into the town,
bounced off the Church then dragged the ground
   and crashed into the abandoned Armory.

Irv Fugman at Vanilla Plump's Ice Cream Shoppe

You know you have a hot summer day in store
    when the line for Ice Cream goes around the block
    before they open in the morning at ten o'clock
and at the front, Irv slumped against the door.

Human nature, on its best day, is ugly,
    when muggy, sticky and hot, it doesn't improve
    so when they finally opened and Irv didn't move,
the vulgus began their usual atrocities.

The third guy in line punched the second who then hit
the woman with the fart face and crooked tits
    who grabbed the wrong guy by the balls who bit her friend

who shoved her labradoodle into his rear-end
until the dog died and gunshots were fired
    and they flung Irv through the window of Mavis Tires.

Irv Fugman at the Conference of Concerned Mothers

Gang violence, poverty, school shootings,
   being dead himself, Irv seemed to imply
   by his bland confidence and magisterial pride,
 that the argument itself was quite beyond disputing

noting, as one of the experts on the rostrum,
   that the best evidence we have today
   now suggests the only effective way
to keep children safe is by killing them.

Mothers rarely are persuaded by the science
and, countering with their own disgorge of violence,
   tore out the seats of the Convention Hall,

tossed them at the speakers and rushed the stage
and in a hot, bare-breasted rampage,
   trampled Irv then crushed him against the wall.

Irv Fugman at the Estate Sale of Walburga Flatz

It was the estate sale of Mrs. Walburga Flatz,
    a woman once known for her fulsome shapes and glamour,
    who, after years of collecting, had a grand *wunderkammer*,
with an unfortunate predilection for porcelain cats

in addition to the twelve living articles roaming the place
    who apostolic gathered in Irv Fugman's lap,
    slouched in a chair, to all take a nap
with one Norwegian Forest cat sitting on his face.

Despite his rather unpleasant state of decease
two rival lawyers considered Irv a masterpiece
    and got into such a heated bidding war

that soon both were wrestling on the floor,
someone pulled a gun and shot Irv in the head,
    everyone returned fire and nine people were dead.

A Mystification of Appalling Dimensions

The whole frustrating mess was too ridiculous,
  no one could figure out how Irv got around,
  why one dead body could not be found,
unless he had a skateboard or some fat accomplice

and the murmurs all suggested that accomplice was me
  because I have nothing better to do with myself
  than drag a rancid corpse all over Hell
to be arrested for riots, loss of life and damaged property.

How I *enjoy* being cursed at, shoved into the copier and punched
and never mind the fact that I worked through lunch
  and have been on the phone all friggin day,

despite having the company dock my pay,
following every lead, psychic vision and crank call
  to bury this wormy bastard once and for all.

The Electric Moonlight in Hell

I am in the Autumn Division, the Night Platoon.
  I transport souls in the service of memories.
  Drink from our wells, display in our breeze
that draws along the roof our soft orange moon.

Every wish, every hope and dream we create
  is the sweet delight that wholly consumes
  the soul dancing by its true parfum
for the love that's lovely, the doom too late.

The Electric Moonlight in Hell
is a popular disco locals know well
   for the Scaffold dancers, the poem at the door,

and under a three-ton Chandelier,
Irv and Dot danced like a happy sneer,
   in Vesuvian confetti, on a black seashore.

Irv Fugman at the LKC Rottweiler Skills Competition

At the Lentil Kennel Club's Annual Competition,
   the top twenty Rottweilers of the county
   were vying for the coveted *Metzgerhund* Trophy
based on intellect, breed characteristics and disposition

with a new and exciting showcase for the breed,
   an all-Rottweiler period production
   of *Julius Caesar*, directed by Martin Gudgeon
and, to my exasperation, Irv Fugman in the lead.

Acts One and Two were cute and amateurish,
and Cassisus kept wandering off to play
   with a stuffed panda or purple tennis ball

but then the assassination scene flipped a switch
and in a Roman orgy of violence and affray
   Irv was torn to pieces and handlers were mauled.

Mrs. Irv Fugman's Days of Scalding Wrath

That should have been the end of Irv Fugman, of course,
   but my life just doesn't seem to work that way
   because, in the newspapers the very next day,
Irv was on the front page in a sensational divorce.

No one notified this office of a wife or next of kin
   and when I took a closer look, I knew this woman,
   thirty years his junior, was not Mrs. Fugman
but my ex-wife trying to grab another fortune.

Reconstituted in his funeral suit,
Irv sat there in the courtroom agog and mute
   while my ex-wife accused him of abuse and affairs

and with familiar tears, dudgeon and sanctimony,
she was awarded his Hummels, his Yugo, alimony
   and his stake in Kubla Cola, at two hundred shares.

Irv Fugman at the Cheerleading Super Nationals

Am I callous, stupid or otherwise irrational
   to ask if everyone in Lentil County is touched in the head?
   Can *no one* see that Irv Fugman is dead?!
Is the world colluding to break my beautiful balls?

At Cheer Nationals held at the Lentil Athletic Court,
   Dynamo Cheer planned a spectacular routine
   that includes, for the first time, the use of trampolines,
a special dispensation to add excitement to the sport.

A Basket Toss, a Right Punch that became a High V,
a Heel Stretch, a Scorpion and then a Liberty
   that Irv executed with surprising verve and grace

til he collided with Brandi while they were trampolining,
they tangled in the banner that tore from the ceiling
   and crashed into the pyro that set fire to the place.

A Moment of Personal Frankness

You might wonder why I'm still employed,
   why The Lentil County Gallows in the square
   doesn't display me naked hanging there
or why my sexual organs haven't been destroyed,

last year I was mauled by my Boss' malamute
   on *Bring Your Pet to Work Day* and since
   my face is frozen in its shitting squints
and I've yet to decide on bringing a lawsuit.

I don't know where the path to Heaven lies
or the tribulations that gird a Paradise,
   I have not found the treasures of faith, the beauty of love,

but in my sad and lonely nights driving around
with sandwich and thermos tracking Irv down
   I've seen in my heart that death is not enough.

Irv Fugman at Donny Brooks' Roller Derby Jammerdrome

This was a rivalry of tits and muscle and hate,
   a semi-final clash between the Delta Valley Napalm
   and the over fifty girls of the Iron City Bombs
with Irv as a Napalm girl on skates.

Irv was the center of a fierce, unbreakable wall
   that shut down every jammer, locking arms
   with Bunny Cannon and Knuckleduster Charms,
a big, turgid superstar in the middle of a brawl

but when they tried to do a Delta Valley Hip Whip
to pick up points at the end of the second quarter
   Irv, floppy and facing the wrong way, tripped

which sent Jammer Chelsea over the rail
into a lighting rig where she was impaled
   panicking the crowd into trampling and slaughter.

Irv Fugman at the Yum Yum Plenty Massage Parlor

The gentlemen visiting the Yum Yum Plenty Massage Parlor
   seemed suspicious to the ladies at the local Assembly of God
   which brought a sting operation by the County Vice Squad
just as Irv Fugman tumbled through the door.

Irv was a mess. The promoters did a number on his face
   and roller derby, riots, death were equally unkind
   to his tired, bloated body, if not his mind,
and the cabbie that dropped him off recommended the place.

With flash-bangs and sting balls, Vice rushed inside
as naked men and Chinese girls did all they could to hide
   or escaped through windows as best as they were able

but in the tumult and confusion, Irv's massage table
burst through a side door and rolled down the street
   masturbated by Hong Li with her supple feet.

Irv Fugman at Adventure Acres Amusement Park

The massage table rolled through the astonished town,
  past the laundromat, a Bake Sale, around the planetarium,
  through the bank, a carwash, then right through the aquarium
to the spastic delight of the first graders of Mrs Brown

and eventually came to rest at its final destination,
 the Roller Coaster known as Thunder Loops of Fear
 where Hong Li dismounted and nakedly disappeared
into the gawping crowd to avoid Immigration.

Irv was thrown out of a loop four cars back
landing on a Belgian woman who had a heart attack,
  closing the Park indefinitely;

meanwhile, over at the Department of the Dead
we somehow buried the wrong man instead
  and were called to court to face the District Attorney...

An Apology from the Department of the Dead
(at the Lentil County Courthouse, the Hon. Eglis T. Schickles presiding)

Your Honor, we're so very glad Mr. Krugman survived,
  the Department is sick with grief and appalled,
   we are as eager to get to the bottom of it all,
it's not regular we bury the wrong person alive

and by that we certainly don't mean to say
  that it's regular to bury the right person alive
   though a few of us would like to do so to our wives
but, of course, that's not why we're gathered here today.

I apologize to Merv Krugman for the clerical oversight
that got him buried alive for fourteen nights
  if he can hear me in his catatonic state;

I hope in time, if not entirely forgetting,
he can overcome his screaming and bedwetting,
  his divorce is easy and his dotage sedate...

21

The Desperation of Desperate Matters

Half the Department was fired, half are being sued.
  The Vice President killed himself, the mayor resigned.
  I already know how important it is to find
the asshole Irv Fugman, I don't need attitude.

What the Hell do people think I'm doing all day?
  It's only slowing me down when they're crying and abusive,
  I have no idea why Irv Fugman is so elusive,
please enlighten me as to how he's getting away.

I flew in a famous sketch artist from Switzerland,
I even asked the Boy Scouts to lend a hand
  searching the woods, the playgrounds, the brothels and bars,

copters are using military-grade radar,
kennel clubs and dog pounds have released their hounds,
  there's dog shit everywhere they're trying to track him down.

The Hell All Over Lentil County

After I got in trouble for all the dog shit
    and the sexual addictions of Boy Scout Troop 14
    I decided to call in the United States Marines
who made a total Gog and Magog out of it.

Their A-10 Warthogs were strafing everything in sight.
    Anyone who even *looked like* they may be dead
    was getting a platoon of tanks upside their head
and the downtown shops were on fire every night.

I'm pretty sure the problem isn't me, it's Irv.
But if anyone in this damned department deserves
    to be slapped in the face and thrown down the stairs

it's the guys at the top who do nothing but complain,
take four hour lunches with steak and champagne
    and only come to the office to have affairs.

Irv Fugman at the Lentil County Tour of Champions

Even though half the county was burned down and gone,
  they decided to proceed with the Annual Bicycle Race
  that starts at the rubble that once was Froggie's Place
and ends by the crater that once was Pam's Salon.

This year, of course, we fielded a much smaller group
  but were hoping that this little event could
  provide us with some respite and some good
but the starting gun drew fire from the twitchy troops.

After the dead bicyclists were collected and thrown away,
this year's Tour of Champions got under way
  and sped through the streets to cheers and horns and flags

but in a tight peloton over shelled out terrain
Irv Fugman got tangled in his bicycle chain
  and we finally got him, and the rest, in body bags.

The Final Repose of Irv Fugman

God and I absolutely had enough of this bullshit.
  I tied Irv Fugman to the grille of my car
  and drove him myself to the fucking graveyard
and threw him in the hole and said, *Bury it.*

When the Reverend came with his girls to give a eulogy
  I punched him in the face and told him to shut his mouth
  and let them all know that if Irv Fugman got out
I wouldn't hesitate at all to kill everybody.

I half expected Irv Fugman to be sitting at my desk,
big and ghoulish, stupid and grotesque,
  although that qualifies him to be upper management...

May God now forget the dead and blest,
give us poor souls on Earth our milk and rest
  and guide us through the blisses of our derangement.

TUCKFORD BUNNY PRESS

Thank you for reading!

Visit us at www.TuckfordBunnyPress.com for all of our delightful books!

www.ingramcontent.com/pod-product-compliance
Lightning Source LLC
Chambersburg PA
CBHW071800020426
42331CB00008B/2347